THE
HAND THAT CAUSES CHAOS IN CHURCHES

THE TARES AND THE WHEAT

THE
HAND THAT CAUSES CHAOS IN CHURCHES

THE TARES AND THE WHEAT

PASTOR TOMICA SCOTT

Glimpse of Glory
CHRISTIAN BOOK PUBLISHING

TABLE OF CONTENTS

ACKNOWLEDGEMENTS

I would like to acknowledge my Lord and Savior, Jesus Christ. He has been my help in every way that I can imagine. The love that He has given me is great. I honor You, my Lord.

With sincere gratitude, I would like to thank my father and mother, Willie and Jewel Daniels, for all the love and support they both have given to me during the good and the bad times.

My children, Leah, Lisa, Mario, and my grandson Jeremiah, I appreciate all the love they have shown me. Thank you all for pressing through with me on my journey of completing my book.

My siblings, Ben, Zizetta, Theresa, Shelisa, Tim, and Dee-Dee, and my nieces and nephews, I love you all.

My spiritual father and mother, Apostle Fred and Prophetess Naomi Louis, I love you both. You all are the best.

I would like to thank Pastor Yolanda Nickerson for seeing the greatness in me and for helping my dream come true.

I would like to thank Pastor Patricia Carroll for your support.

All of my friends, loved ones, supporters and all the saints of God, I love each and every one of you.

INTRODUCTION

In these perilous times, we are seeing so much happening worldwide, even when it comes to the church. You might be thinking, "What church?" Well, there are things the devil will do to cause evil and chaos in some churches. You see, we are seeing good and evil on the rise, and it comes from a source that is not of flesh and blood. The Bible tells us,"For we wrestle not against flesh and blood, but against principalities, against powers, against the rulers of the darkness of this world, against spiritual wickedness in high places" (Ephesians 6:12-KJV). So, even though flesh and blood are being used, it is the replica of what is happening in the spirit realm. There are powers that have captured the minds and hearts of individuals and have caused them to see the life of the unseen. Some people have taken on the characters of unclean and evil spirits, and those spirits have been in operation in the church world.

Some churches have a certain image that they want people who join to bow down to. The Bible speaks of a prophet named Daniel who was about to be murdered because he would not bow down and worship a false god image. The Bible also speaks of tares and wheat and how they will grow together in the last days (Matthew, Chapter 13-KJV). To help you understand better, in short, wheat represents good and tares represent bad and evil. Many cannot tell the difference. One writer said, "While growing next to wheat, tares cannot be distinguished from the real wheat. It is not until near the time of harvest that you can discern which of the two is the real item." There are some people who represent wheat and some who represent tares, and one way to know the difference between them is by the fruit that they bear (Matthew, Chapter 7-KJV).

There is also a war between the Kingdom of God and the kingdom of darkness. And a system has been created for both of them to operate. This war has spilled over into the natural realm, so that is why some people are confused about who is who, and what is real and what is fake and what is good and what is evil. I want you to know who is at work here: the devil himself. He can and will literally use people to do his evil work.

This book will help you understand the characteristics of some people (including spiritual leaders) who profess to be a part of the body of Christ and go to church, but they will succumb to the devil and carry out his evil tactic. Remember, some of them represent wheat and some represent tares. This book will take you on a journey and give you a clear view of the hand that causes chaos in churches.

CHAPTER ONE
THE HAND THAT CAUSES CHAOS IN CHURCHES

1 Corinthians 14:33
For God is not the author of confusion, but of peace, as in all churches of saints.

In some churches we are not seeing the hand of God nor are we experiencing the peace of God like we supposed to. What I mean by this is that when a person goes to a church, whether they are a member or a visitor, they should be able to feel peace, love, joy, positive energy and they should also be able to gain strength from not only the message the pastor teaches or preaches, but they should also be able to gain strength from other parishioners of that church, too. When these things are displayed by all the members of a church, then there is a clear indication that the presence of God is there, and His hand is resting upon that church. It also shows those who are unsaved that we Christians do not just go to church, but we are the church. When there is confusion, strife, deception, backbiting, gossiping, witchcraft, and other negative things taking place in a church, especially if carried out by a spiritual leader, one will not feel the presence of God nor His hand resting upon that church.

Now as I shared before, there is the Kingdom of God and the kingdom of darkness. I want to make sure that you understand which one Christians should represent. What's more is that God has assigned certain spiritual leaders (clergy) to churches who have His heart and is anointed to teach, to preach, to pray for, to spiritually develop and equip, and to lead the members of their church according to His plan. (Read Jeremiah 3:15 and Romans 8:30.) When church members are spiritually equipped, it helps them grow and come together in unity and they will also have knowledge of who the Son of God is: Jesus Christ. On the other hand, when a person who God has not assigned or given His heart to is at the helm of a church, even though they may have certain gifts (Romans 11:29), they can easily find themselves operating in a system that represents the kingdom of darkness, and the spirit in which they are operating in can spill over into the lives of some of their members, especially those who may not be spiritually mature concerning the Word of God and the things of Him.

There are many spiritual leaders who say they are called by God. They are operating in skills but not under the anointing of God. Some of them are considered modern-day Pharisees who are only setting up spiritual gates and opening portals for demonic activity to invade the minds and the hearts of the members of their church as well as nonmembers. The Pharisees in the Bible were members of a religious group or party that frequently clashed with Jesus Christ over His interpretation of the Law. Some of these kinds of leaders have partnered with Satan to ensnare souls and it has caused a great falling away. The Bible clearly warns us that the falling away will come (2 Thessalonians 2:1-3-NIV).

I find that the lack of "the teaching or revelation of Christ" is the reason people are receiving lies, and this very thing has been a door opening for Satan's plans. We must acknowledge who the real enemy is that is causing chaos. Let me go a little deeper so that you may understand where I am going with this. The enemy has come in and sown tares in some churches, even

12

in some of the churches the Lord has planted and assigned great, anointed leaders in. Satan enters some churches to create a system within a system. Satan wanted to be just like God before the beginning of time. I believe when he was kicked out of Heaven (Revelations 12:7-10), he developed plans to work through people who would succumb to his plans, to destroy you. The people (tares) he uses will look just like you (wheat) in the natural but are naturally and spiritually dangerous. They are just like a dead man's bones.

TAKEAWAYS AND PERSONAL NOTES FOR SPIRITUAL GROWTH

_____

_____

_____

_____

_____

_____

_____

_____

_____

_____

_____

_____

_____

_____

_____

_____

_____

_____

_____

_____

_____

_____

CHAPTER TWO

THE WORKS OF THE FLESH

Galatians 5:19-2-ESV
Now the works of the flesh are evident: sexual immorality, impurity, sensuality, idolatry, sorcery, enmity, strife, jealousy, fits of anger, rivalries, dissensions, divisions, envy, drunkenness, orgies, and things like these. I warn you, as I warned you before, that those who do such things will not inherit the kingdom of God.

We must understand that our flesh is a tool the devil will use against us. As a matter of fact, the flesh is one of the main tools he has used to build his kingdom of darkness. Galatians 5:19-2 shows us the characteristic of Satan. Some of the works of the flesh this Scripture lists are carried out by many spiritual leaders as well as others. Some spiritual leaders, including those who are pastors of a church, are caught in the craftiness of their flesh and if they are not delivered in the early stage of Salvation, it can easily reveal itself in a later stage when they are striving to develop.

1 John 2:16-ESV declares, "For all that is in the world, the lust of the flesh, the lust of the eyes, and the pride of life, is not of the Father but from the world." The lust of the flesh, the eyes, and the pride of life have taken over some churches. Lust is one of the reasons we are seeing sexual perversion, theft, false teaching, manipulation, lies, gossiping, sowing discord against others, witchcraft, deception and the spirit of control

17

fully operating in some churches. Some church buildings are used to sell illegal drugs, for sex trafficking, and prostitution, which has caused some spiritual leaders to use their position and authority to have sex with the opposite sex, same-sex, and even children.

The lust of the flesh is in your members, as some mature Christians might say, and it operates from your heart. Some spiritual leaders who do not have a heart of God nor committed to "staying in tune with Him" and doing what He instructs them to do and say would rather fulfill their own lustful desires and purposes. When they do these things, it can have an adverse effect on the lives of the members of their church. You see, the lust of the flesh is being displayed by people who are saved and unsaved, those who are in the world and of the world, and they operate in the world system, as some mature Christians might say. We Christians are in the world, but we are not supposed to be of the world and operating in the world system. 1 John 2:15-KJV tells us Christians to "Love not the world, neither the things that are in the world. If any man loves the world, the love of the Father is not in him."

Some spiritual leaders whose motives are not pure are very dangerous. Some of them do not know how dangerous it is for them to get caught up in the things of the world, because they believe what they are doing is right. They are on an assignment to destroy everything and anyone to get what their flesh desires. They are hiding in the pulpit, tent revivals, conferences, and gatherings, and some of them may reside in the same home as you. They will preach sermons at church week after week, and their messages come from their own heart and not from the throne of God. They are not hearing anything from God. They are scamming you out of your money, time, and life. Yes, they are planting you in a ground that is not fertile. These spiritual leaders study how to cause their desires to come to the forefront. They rely on keeping those around them, including the members of their church, in darkness. The devil takes these kinds of leaders and magnifies their views, perverts their dreams through imaginative thoughts, which causes them to desire images that are not God's plan. Their minds are blinded. They are seeing images that seem to carry glory, but it is a false glory.

These kinds of spiritual leaders have become content with operating from a place of selfishness and greed. The devil keeps them in a place of wanting more so that they may stay hungry for the things of this chaotic world, while never really growing spiritually. The reason the devil has repeatedly used them is because they have not denied their fleshly desires, and it has brought so many of them down over the years. "Pride goes before destruction" (Proverbs 16:18-KJV). It has caused some of them who pastors a church to be forced to resign from their church. It has caused some of them to face divorces. It has caused some of them to experience financial lack. Also, because of some of their sinful acts, it has caused some of their members to carry out some of those same sinful acts. It has caused some of their members to experience "church hurt." It has caused some of their members to experience confusion and unease in the spirit. It has caused some of their members to become spiritually stagnant. And, it has even caused some of their members to turn against God. You may be someone who has experienced this from a church, or you may know someone else who has experienced this from their church.

I want you to understand that our flesh is our studio of failure, so at all costs we must rid ourselves of the ungodly desires of our flesh and the ungodly things that we can easily be tempted with in this world. The Bible tells us that temptation comes from our own desires, which entice us and drag us away (James 1:14-NLT). The reason there is so much chaos in some churches is because of some of the leaders and some of the members lustful desires. It is always best to know who the real enemy is. There are too many people who do not know the difference between the tares and the wheat, and many of them are experiencing spiritual death because of their lack of knowledge. I want you to understand that God never intended for spiritual leadership to be corrupt, yet many are corrupt.

TAKEAWAYS AND PERSONAL NOTES FOR SPIRITUAL GROWTH

_____

_____

_____

_____

_____

_____

_____

_____

_____

_____

_____

_____

_____

_____

_____

_____

_____

_____

_____

_____

_____

CHAPTER THREE
THE KINDS OF SPIRITUAL LEADERS

Matthew 22:14-KJV
For many are called, but few are chosen.

Ephesian 4:11-12-GNT
It was he (God) who "gave gifts to people"; he appointed some to be apostles, some to be prophets, others to be evangelists, others to be pastors and teachers. He did this to prepare all God's people for the work of Christian service, in order to build up the body of Christ.

SPIRITUAL LEADERS WHO ARE CALLED AND CHOSEN BY GOD

If a spiritual leader is called and chosen by God, they will exhibit the fruit of the Spirit. "The fruit of the Spirit is love, joy, peace, longsuffering, gentleness, goodness, faith, meekness, and temperance" (Galatians 5:22-23-KJV). The fruit of the Spirit is essential for one to be able to love beyond the things they see. When a spiritual leader has the fruit of the Spirit, it will reveal their character and level of maturity, and it will also determine how well they can lead. A called and chosen leader is concerned about their physical being, their soul, and their growth in God as well as those who they are called to lead. They are not selfish or afraid. They display true discipleship because they care about the best interest of others and their

23

spiritual growth. They are not money hungry or hungry for membership. They are committed to teaching the truth to their members as well as others they may come in contact with. They always have a fresh word to deliver because they are constantly in the presence of God. Sound doctrine is what they preach. They are firm and passionate. They will not accommodate your sins or emotions, but rather tell you the truth in love. They will help you become mature and push you into the place you are called to be. They are seeking the heart of God to make sure they are righteous and in good standing with the Father. They are prayer warriors which means they are constantly praying and watching out for you in the spirit.

These kinds of leaders will move by the power of the Holy Spirit, and when you are around them, you began to see God in them and their actions. They are fearless and hopeful, full of God, and will fight in the spirit to protect what belongs to God. They don't try to deceive anyone or covet what belongs to another person. Rather, they speak more blessings upon the lives of others. They are not into witchcraft like the tares or leaders that have lost their power and now turning to an evil power source. They understand that God wants nothing but the best for you and that He will never put you in danger. They will not stone you, but they will exercise their authority in love and in the spirit of humility.

As I shared before, God will give you a leader after His own heart to help develop you into a mature son or daughter of the Kingdom of God. God desires compassion to be in full effect so when this kind of leader speaks the truth, the Word of God that comes out of his or her mouth will be accepted and will purify individuals if they allow it to. You will see true advancements in every area of your life when you are a member of a church where there is a leader who has been called and chosen by God.

24

You will receive your spiritual inheritance when you have a true leader. If you have this kind of leader at the helm of the church that you attend, you should continue praying for them and supporting them as they continue to advance the Kingdom of God.

Now let me share with you some of the things I have seen in leadership when it comes to leaders who are called by God. They have elevated the Kingdom of God as He has instructed them to do. I have seen some of them pour out of their hearts, yet they have been taken advantage of. I have also learned that leaders who truly have the heart of God are not going to put you in danger because God is leading them.

SPIRITUAL LEADERS THAT REPRESENT TARES

God did not call or choose some leaders who are currently holding a position at some churches. These kinds of leaders can and will easily serve as the tares, and Satan is the one who has planted them in some churches. Matthew 13:25-26 describes how the enemy sowed tares. I have seen and heard of some of these kinds of leaders who have gone to some churches with an agenda to take over. It is crazy how some of them can be so infuriated by the growth and the authority another leader has, to the point that they will have them removed from their position or even killed. Satan has used methods to slander the reputation of some of the leaders who have been called by God. Evil is happening all around us, and it is even worse when it happens in some churches. Sadly, as I shared before, many people do not know how to distinguish those who represent tares and those who represent wheat. The love has even waxed cold just as the Bible tells us in Matthew 24:12-KJV.

You must realize that the tares are in operation because Satan needs to have workers to fulfill his mission. Many people have been marked for his purpose, just as Judas (who betrayed Jesus Christ) was, but that is why God decided to die for everyone. I want you to understand that there is no way of getting around the place that we have arrived at, but you can continue allowing God to do His work in you; that will cause you to be shown as one that is of His Kingdom, not of the kingdom of darkness.

Your work says a lot about you. This is going to cause great conflict because the enemy wants to win. There are demonic powers that are working strongly in those who represent the tares to cause chaos in the life of those who are of God, but you must have the willingness to continue doing good on your journey. The tares in leadership are sent to harm, to deceive, and to draw an individual away from knowing the truth. These leaders are in the churches masquerading as being anointed and sent by God, and they are preying on babes in Christ. I would like to remind you that the Bible speaks of how the devil sent messengers to baffle the apostle Paul, and he will do the same concerning you. Satan is still on a journey to destroy whoever he can, especially Christians.

Some leaders who are not called by God are highly educated in the Word of God and excellent in doing the work of the ministry, just like the Pharisees were. They wanted all eyes to be on them. They had religious ceremonies but never knew God. Everything is on point when it comes to them. They will equip you with the tools to use the gift that God has placed inside of you, and help you develop a substantial life outside of ministry but never bringing you into a place of being set free. I am a firm believer in doing everything excellent when it comes to God, but there must be a godly life one is living behind their success. I want you to know that the devil can only equip you with that of the natural because he is not able to spiritually help you elevate in a kingdom he is not from. These leaders have literally given themselves over to ancient spirits who are giving them knowledge and information about you and the things that pertain to the kingdom of this world. You will only benefit from the natural realm, which comes with a price. This kind of scheme is how deception has crept in. Blessings are being foreseen as natural things. Blessings are not just those things of the natural but also of the spirit. These leaders are sent to distract you and they are fully loaded with what is of their kind.

1 Corinthians 2:4-5-NIV declares, "My message and my preaching were not in persuasive words of wisdom but in demonstration of the Spirit's power, so that your faith would not rest on human wisdom but God's power." When the enemy tempted Jesus, it was all the things that pertained to this world. Your desires, if not pure, will open doors for you to be a prey to these kinds of leaders. You will not grow spiritually and for some, they will not grow naturally. Everybody is not going to be rich; I do not care how close the resource is. There is always a price to pay when leaders that are sown are allowed to be in a position of authority. These kinds of leaders will sow seeds of discord and it will destroy the trust in their congregation. There is so much drama in some churches. The Word of the Lord tells us that those that practice such works, will not inherit the Kingdom of God (1 Corinthians 6:9-NIV). Such leaders have evil in their hearts, and they are only sent on assignment to draw you into darkness, deceiving, and being deceived, and they are sowing because they were sown—and they understand the importance of sowing. They are watchers that do not sleep but rather watch you in the spirit and plan and carry out their

next deceptive move. They are just waiting to carry out some evil tactic against you.

Because some people have the gift of discernment, they can sense when something is not right, but they can and will still ignore any warning signs after years of being under the spell of these kinds of spiritual leaders that they have adapted to. It becomes a way of life for them. When you continue sitting under this kind of spiritual leader, your spirit will continue to be fed and filled with contamination. They can assault you in the spirit without you being fully aware of it. These leaders have watched the seed they planted inside of you grow. After a while, you can find yourself becoming just like them because you can "become what you eat."

I want you to understand that these leaders (tares) grew with us (wheat). They learned the characteristics of what church was supposed to be like, and because they are the devil's advocates, they know what is of them and who is of their kind. They were sown but learned through the behaviors of those that were not spiritually delivered from certain things and by this they were able to grow and have no restriction. For years, some leaders have presented themselves to be holy, just as God told us to be holy as He is holy (1 Peter 1:26), but they have been conducting and living a lifestyle opposite of what they have been teaching and preaching. They have been promiscuous, they have a lying tongue, they have sown discord, they are gossipers, and have even had some gossiping mothers in their church. 1 Corinthians 15:33 tells us about corrupt communication, which is in essence the same as gossiping.

The things I have listed are just a few peas in the pot to show you how their actions have mirrored the devil's. Now we are seeing the whole stew in the pot, with extra flavor. Spiritual leaders who have not been delivered from sinful things do not have room to say anything to anyone else who is sinning, and actually some of them are afraid to say anything because they got a bag and the bones. Their actions will manifest what is within them. These leaders have taken over some churches and they manipulated the atmosphere within those churches. The spirit of Jezebel and divination has entered those churches, and as a result of this, some leaders within those same churches are timid. Some of us may refer to them as weak and timid. Timid leaders have taken a seat in the back of some of those churches, under the pew. Someone, somewhere, please call 911. This has become a spiritual emergency, literally.

I know that I shared a lot concerning these kinds of leaders, but I wanted to ensure you that I have dealt with the issues surrounding them and how their behavior and teachings can easily spill over into the lives of those who are members of the churches they lead. The weakness of the flesh has even had the minds of them that supposed to be saved darkened. These leaders have had full access to operate in a form of godliness but denying the power and so are those that say the name of the Lord, yet they are still compromising. (Read 2 Timothy 3:5.) They cannot hear or see what God is doing but are telling you what the Lord is saying. Which Lord is speaking?

They look just like you and me, but they are an enemy to the cross of Jesus Christ. They have indulged in so many things that are not Christ-like. The Bible tells us that a little leaven leavens the whole lump (Galatians 5:9-NKV). These kinds of leaders need to repent and turn from their wicked ways. They need to be taught how to lead by godly example, and some of you who have set under their leadership and taken on some of their ways, need to be taught all over again. Hebrews 5:12 declares, "For though by this time, you ought to be teachers, you need someone to teach you again the first principles of the oracles of God; and you have come to need milk and not solid food."

If you are of the kingdom of darkness it will show, and if you are of God, it will show. A tree is known for its fruits. This is how you will know the difference between the tares and the wheat. Finally, once you come into full knowledge of knowing we are all just passing through this world and we are not a part of this world or the worldly system, then the faster we will adapt to our God-given purpose and realize what we do for Him is the most important thing we could ever do. We must also realize that this worldly system was never created for us Christians, but it was created for the dead.

TAKEAWAYS AND PERSONAL NOTES FOR SPIRITUAL GROWTH

CHAPTER FOUR
DECEPTION IN LEADERSHIP

2 Thessalonians 2:3-NIV
Do not let anyone deceive you in any way...

Galatians 6:6-8
Do not deceive yourselves; no one makes a fool of God. People will reap exactly what they sow. If they sow in the field of their natural desires, from it they will gather the harvest of death; if they sow in the field of the Spirit, from the Spirit they will gather the harvest of eternal life.

I pastored for a few years in a small town. I must say that warfare and carrying the burden alone was very heartbreaking. I honestly would have never thought that, being a pastor, I would encounter such hostile treatment. Dealing with opposition in my marriage at that time, along with ministry, was overwhelming. How could anyone escape the pain of being overloaded with ministry work, laboring with enemies on your team and in your household at the same time? I was fighting enemies on every hand. Many of you might be in a position in ministry where you are fighting assigned enemies from every angle, too. You might be battling witches that are working the craft of speaking curses against everything you do, and they are looking to see you fail and not be who God has called you to be.

I must expose the situation that I encountered to help set someone free. I was under attack in ministry from day one by the team assigned to me. Moving to this town was exciting for me because I was somewhere new with someone who I thought loved me. We married and started a ministry. Of course, this was exciting, but it came with great responsibility, and I was ready to tackle it head-on. I love God and His people and had the lifestyle to back it up. I was unafraid and unashamed to do what God wanted me to do. Months passed, and I began to see the string of jealousy and dislike toward me in those who said, "I am with you, pastor." Whenever there is evilness in the heart of anyone, it will manifest when an opponent is before them, and to them I was trouble for the ministry. They did not want me to preach the truth to them but wanted me to burn the members and others outside the four walls of our church. When it was my time to preach, they would sit on me and cause a great distraction while I ministered but wanted me to amen them and back them up whenever they preached. Some spiritual leaders who are called and chosen by God can have a secret assassin sleeping with them every night, watching them in the spirit realm.

My home was a mess. Everyone thought it was together and that is how it is with many who may have similar stories. You can be married, have a ministry together, and the two of you can be gifted and anointed and in the eyes of the people, it looks great, but behind the closed doors of the church and your home, there is an enemy. These kinds of wars give off bad signals to those that are in ministry and it causes chaos in the church. No one should every have to see leaders fighting and tearing down each other but because tares have grown with us, this is the issue. No one would have ever thought that Cain and Abel came from the same parents. (Genesis, Chapter 4). Naturally, they did but Abel had a heart that was for God, while Cain was the first fruits of evil. This is a replica of what the wheat and tares are.

When you think of leadership, you think of someone that is honest, loyal, and dedicated to the call they have accepted. Never in life would you think that it could be those in leadership that are cunning and deceptive. I know it is hard to even imagine that you would suffer at the hands of those that say they love God. I am going to show you the different factors that are at work in leadership so that there will be a clear understanding of what is at hand. Before I go into details about these factors, I am going to share my testimony so that you will understand the purpose of me writing this chapter.

I have been in ministry for over 20 years and I never thought I would experience the pain, lies, shame, and mistreatment that I have in ministry. I was raised in Texas, a place where you must be saved for real or the people will not accept you. I mean Texas will stone you in the middle of service if you are false. The Texas slogan, " Don't mess with Texas," is real. It is okay to laugh out loud. While I was growing up in God, I had a great leader that shielded me and taught me the true meaning of what it was to be saved. She taught me the word and helped me give birth to my prayer life. She took time to watch me grow spiritually and she allowed me to minister in church service. I learned what true servanthood is while serving under her leadership. I learned that by cleaning bathrooms, working in the kitchen, and teaching the youth. Even as I began to progress in ministry, I still served. The Bible says, "The greatest among you shall be your servant" (Matthew 23:11-KJV). Years went by and my name started surfacing in Texas. The word got out that I was a young prophet in the city. I started connecting with other leaders and getting invites to go to their churches and preach, which is something very exciting for young ministers.

35

"As a young leader, you have so much zeal and you are ready to take the devil's head off everywhere," is what someone said.

As a southern Church of God in Christ girl, I had no idea what was coming. I was a pure green horn. As the connections came, so did the deception. The first deceptive encounter I had was at the age of twenty-three. A prophet invited me to a church to be the keynote speaker, and I was overly excited. I was studying the Word of God for hours just to make sure I had everything together. I arrived at the church and found out the pastor of that church did not even know I was coming, so this alerted me that I was not the keynote speaker for the hour. The prophet that invited me told them to give me ten minutes to speak and with me being a young minister, I obeyed and took the ten minutes to speak. When I opened my mouth, God spoke through me and the pastor of that church rejoiced when God had me to speak over his life. He was literally at the brink of death, but God used me to declare that years would be added to his life. God used me to preach and prophesy within that ten minutes. The prophet that invited me had planned to speak the same message. When that prophet got up to preach, there was nothing for him to say, so they proceeded to raise money.

I was literally hurt by this because this was actually the first encounter I had with a lying prophet and it was my first opportunity to be a keynote speaker. His agenda was to invite me so that he could raise money because he knew a crowd would follow me. Can I tell you that what the devil meant for evil God turned it around for my good? Even though the spirit of deception is on the loose in some churches, we must be wise. This was the first time I had experienced something like this and it most certainly was not the last time I experienced something like this. Over the years, I have noticed that the spirit of deception in some churches has increased. Facing these encounters has compelled me to expose the devil, not people. I want you to realize that it is the devil that uses people to carry out his schemes and tactics. He is the real one that is working. My prayer and desire is that no one be deceived by the tricks of the devil. I am intending to destroy every tactic of the devil as it comes my way and make you aware of deception so that you won't be deceived.

According to Google, deception is "the action of deceiving someone." In leadership, deception happens when a leader is open to the kingdom of darkness. Anytime a person is operating in deception, it is merely because they are blinded somewhere. Anytime there is a place that has not been purified, there will be lack. The Bible speaks of King Saul, who was a great example of how individuals in leadership can operate and not reside in God's perfect will. If a leader has space in their life that has not been healed, those wounds can become a lethal weapon against the Kingdom of God. You might be thinking, "What do you mean woman of God?" I want you to know that sin is always a reproach against the Kingdom of God. It is a deadly weapon that allows one to be a slave and slaves will obey their master.

Deception can be very cunning. One must be deceived, to deceive. The Bible declares in 2 Timothy 3:13-NKJV, that "evil men and impostors will grow worse and worse, deceiving and being deceived." Whenever you see spiritual leaders who can see everyone else's wrong but cannot see themselves, they are deceived, and this is a clear indication they were not sent by God. You must be able to see your own sins. Spiritual leaders need to have a heart that is pure in order to lead anyone because what is in their hearts will begin to work through them. "But Pastor, I am not like everyone else. What they are doing is horrible," so you say, but your heart, that is open to the kingdom of darkness can do anything. "The heart is deceitful above all things, and desperately wicked: who can know it?" (Jeremiah 17:9-NKJV.)

Deception in leadership comes in many forms. I want to take my time with this because many people have fallen victim to deception in many ways in leadership. I, as a spiritual leader and a woman of God, have the right to expose the hidden serpents and their illegal weapons that are being used against the Kingdom of God. I have seen how deception has affected the lives of many people who attend church. It has caused many to turn their back on God, many to lose their faith, many to believe that God is not real, and more. Now I am getting ready to get exclusive, so embrace yourself. I have seen the worst of worst of those in leadership that were used by the devil to hold captive the souls of those they were calling out for deliverance.

I have seen leaders who are musicians release demonic powers as they played. I have seen an evil side of leaders that have no power or have lost their power team up with the sorcerers to perform a church service. I have seen leaders that simply were not led by God to put on religious ceremonies and they operated in a gift where they received their information from dark powers. I have even seen delusional methods being applied to services to get people to give money. I have seen individuals use hypnosis in the building. I have seen those who have operated in gifts, and then afterward go and have sex with the same-sex or the opposite sex. I have seen individuals lie and say God said that you are my husband/wife only to have someone help build them a playhouse for lust to operate heavily in their heart. I have seen the tricks of many doing witchcraft rituals in church openly and because the leaders are not led by God, the kingdom of darkness had legal rights to invade. The list goes on and on, and so will I to expose the devil on every hand. Yes, I am going to expose the devil throughout this book.

How are people going to know the truth from a lie unless someone takes a stand?

You see, it is in these stages, when you have leaders who are doing all kinds of evil things, that church hurt occurs, because there is no true presence of God in those churches, but just a form of godliness there. Therefore, the members of those churches are now receiving the working of the flesh in those leaders who have been allowed to lead them. I want you to remember that the tree is known by the fruit it bears. If the tree bears good fruit, you will see good works. There will be manifestation of the power of God and demonstration of His spirit in action. The glory of the Lord will be magnified, and you will have peace. In 1 Corinthians 14:33-NKJV, we are told that "God is not the author of confusion but of peace." Satan is the one that loves confusion, and he loves to be seen. That is why I don't mind exposing him. The devil has destroyed so many lives, and some of us who realize what is happening spiritually don't want to cry aloud against those who are wicked in spiritual leadership positions. (Read Isaiah 58:1). I am going to go deeper in my sharing because I want people to be set free. God did not call me to be a silent prophet. I shall, like the prophet Elijah, expose the devil and let the world know there is a God, and His name is Jesus.

When someone is not sold out to God and their destiny and they decide to take on the role of a spiritual leader, they must understand that they are an open target. They are going to experience major conflict and they will face obstacles. God has called all of us to do something, whether it be pastoring, teaching, evangelism or some other task, but purification is necessary. The role of spiritual leaders consists of having a relationship with God and if married, whoever they have a relationship with, should be made known to those that they consider leading. There should not be any hidden agendas. See, what is in a person will be attracted to them and sent to them. The devil's job is to make, by all means necessary, his kingdom rise above God's Kingdom. When you take on a spiritual leadership role and you have not given your heart to God, just know that you are the illegal lethal weapon used against the church. Accepting and committing to a spiritual leadership position before it is time will cause the devil to be seen and churches will become a mockery. Spiritual leaders must wait on the timing of the Lord with any ministry work they are called to do. A sold-out leader is very vital because God has assigned individuals to hear your voice in this dispensation you are in. Let me make something clear: there is a big difference in a spiritual leader that has a calling on his or her life and has moved without God's approval, and those that are sent on assignment to destroy you. Some spiritual leaders have been called but need deliverance. They will make mistakes because they have not been healed or have not matured enough to handle the assignment. It does not mean that they are going to be lost, but they can certainly cause damage.

On the other hand, those who are sent by Satan are after your soul. They come strictly to invade you with sin and darkness, making sure you never reach your destiny. They come in the name of lies and they have a form of godliness but deny the power thereof. They come to impart wickedness inside of you and bring you down to nothing. They are filled with hatred and want to demolish your soul and those who are connected to you, too. They are intentionally sent for your downfall and would physically kill you if they could. These kinds of leaders will try to build a name for themselves first, so they can draw a crowd. They will come up with all kinds of services to raise money. They are very precise with their word of knowledge because they are receiving information from accent spirits. Some of them want their churches to be able to work in full deception powers. They will even travel from church to church, speaking lies and flattering people with their gifts and talents, and they work witchcraft and perform rituals among people. These individuals are in full operation in serving their god in front of you openly without you knowing it. They teach the doctrine of the devil. They usher in the full manifestation of the power of darkness, ensnaring the souls of those who are weak, and they are working to keep those in captivity who are already overtaken by the enemy. These are the kinds of leaders that must be exposed. While some churches have a problem with exposing them, because they are screaming, "Do not judge," God wants you to be aware of them. Having the spirit of discernment is very critical in this hour and being able to use it will keep you from being tricked by the devil.

Now that we understand deception, let me remind you again that there is the Kingdom of God and the kingdom of darkness. These two kingdoms are currently at war right now and, because of this, there is a heated battle that is taking place. The battle is occurring in the spirit realm, but it is manifesting in the natural realm. And, as I have shared repeatedly in this book, there are the tares and the wheat, and they are growing together (Read Matthew 13:24-30). We must watch and pray, because we are fighting on every side as Jesus did. Not against flesh and blood, but wickedness in high places, just as the Bible tells us in Ephesians 6:12. Jesus had the kingdom of darkness after him to destroy his purpose, and it was the religious synagogue people that were His greatest enemy. This same method has been put into action against us. The assignment of the religious church was to keep individuals from seeing them and never come to the truth. They were ordained by Satan to put yokes upon the people and cause no one to know the true God, but to remain in the condition of being stuck in religion. We are seeing this same tool being used today.

If you are a spiritual leader who have been deceiving people, allow yourself to be healed. The sin in your life will have you committed to a church service, being used illegally, and that sin will become a weapon against those who are being ministered to. You might be thinking, "Being used illegally, How?" or "I know God called me and that is why I started a ministry." God may have called you, but He wants you to be whole. When you are not whole, and you place yourself in a spiritual leadership position before it is time for you to hold such position, it will cause everything to be aborted, including those who you are overseeing and preaching and teaching to. The Bible declares in Isaiah 53:5-KJV, "He was wounded for our transgressions, He was bruised for our iniquities; the chastisement of our peace was upon Him; and by His stripes, we are healed." There is a responsibility to make sure you are healed before coming into operation over God's people. When I say, "healed" I mean healed for real. After you become whole, you will see a difference in your life and you will be able to make a difference in the lives of others. You will begin to mature spiritually.

When God created Adam, he was a mature man. When God sent out His apostles, they were mature men. And when King David became King, he was a mature man. Some may ask, "Well, what are you trying to say here, pastor?" What I am saying is that God is not going to send someone to carry out an assignment when they have not been equipped to do so. The pressures of carrying out that assignment can get them killed. Your life has to be one in which you decide to live for God. You have to get to a place in your life where you can declare with your own mouth, "For God I live and for God I die." That simply means that you are fully committed to Him. A lot of spiritual leaders are ordained by God, and while it is rewarding, it can be dangerous if mishandled. If you are in the position of a spiritual leader, you must literally "die to self." If you are into self, you do not hear God; therefore, you will cause deaths, premature births, hurts, and disruption to the plan of God for someone's life.

TAKEAWAYS AND PERSONAL NOTES FOR SPIRITUAL GROWTH

_____

_____

_____

_____

_____

_____

_____

_____

_____

_____

_____

_____

_____

_____

_____

_____

_____

_____

_____

_____

_____

CHAPTER FIVE

DECEPTION IN MARRIAGES

"Our culture promotes many deceptions that can quickly destroy a marriage." (www.familylife.com)

Colossians 3:17-NIV
And whatever you do, whether in word or deed, do it all in the name of the Lord Jesus, giving thanks to God the Father through him.

Hebrews 13:4
Marriage should be honored by all, and the marriage bed kept pure, for God will judge the adulterer and all the sexually immoral.

I am excited about this chapter, yet anxious to get through it. It will expose the ugly truth of my life. Let me start by sharing that a marriage is a covenant and a soul-tie beyond what many people think. Marriage is a ministry in and of itself, but far too many people do not understand this about marriage. A marriage has no life when there is no prayer and fasting, and when it lacks communication and respect. Some marriages are currently in a dead zone. I want to announce that some things are not like the pretty picture that some have painted in their marriages. There are many struggles in marriages when there are sin issues carried out by one or both spouses. If a person is in ministry, their issues with sin should be dealt with before they become a spiritual leader and even before getting married. If their sin issues are not dealt with prior to marriage, it can break up their home and cause a disaster in that marriage. Every couple has issues, but sin issues can have a detrimental effect on any marriage. I know of some spiritual leaders, who are married, yet they are addicted to pornography, molesting their children, committed to incest, abusive to their spouse and children, and committing adultery or fornicating, and many of them have literally had to watch their spouse be flirtatious with their own family members and those who are appealing to them. These are some of the reasons there are so many divorces. Financial problems are not the major issue as many have continuously stated.

When an opportunity presents itself, whatever is really in a person's heart will begin to manifest. You see, couples who don't usually have anything materialistic are incredibly happy. When you are married, you must be incredibly careful not to allow the devil to create a stem of bitterness in you while trying to stay free in a relationship. You do not know the sacrifice someone else is making just to have sanity. Many couples have been married for years and do not even conversate or have sexual relations, but they will go to church together and present themselves as though everything is fine with them. This thing really runs deep in marriage.

Now, here is something to consider when marrying. The devil will work on both the husband and wife to keep them uneased with each other, and one of his greatest tools is to make both of them think they are right. If Satan can get you to think you are right, you will do whatever it takes to defend yourself. This is simply because there is a low level of maturity. You never have to prove yourself when the evidence is obvious. For some, they know they are wrong but will continue to go as though nothing is wrong because of pride. They will slaughter you until you walk out the door and then get mad when you leave as though you did wrong for wanting better for yourself. God holds a high standard in marriage and ministry because it is supposed to be a replica of what He has designed for Himself and the church. (Read Revelation 21). *God said you are my spouse.* We see this phrase being commonly used in the church to get a spouse.

Now this brings me to what I experienced in a marriage. In this chapter, I am going to expose my truth and the truth of so many other marriages. I am in ministry and I married someone else who was also in ministry. After we got married, we started a church together. While going to church and ministering across the city, there were constant arguments about something never coming into agreement and these fights almost became physical at times. Many married couples who are in ministry work so well together in ministry, but they are falling apart at home. I learned that home issues will spill over into ministry. Those who attend your church will pick up on what is happening at home. It will cause a leader's message to be about their partner instead of God. I realize that there are other people who have gifts just like spiritual leaders who are married, and these people can discern when spouses are not on one accord. Someone once told me that "God will cover your sins and keep people from seeing them." I do believe this but that does not diminish the gift of discernment that some people have. They can easily discern when something is not right in any given situation, and I am certain they discerned things about my marriage.

What I experienced in that marriage was meant to kill me, but it built me. You see, I believed that I was marrying a man of God, my soul mate, just like many of you thought about the person you are with or were with, but in reality, you ended up with someone that was not saved. We must first be alarmed by the schemes of the adversary in marriages. There are many men and women who have been treated so badly by some spiritual leaders that say they are of God. It has caused such calamity and hatred in the hearts of those who have fallen victim to this madness, and many have died both naturally and spiritually. I had fallen victim to this kind of marriage, and it hurt some of those who attended my church.

When you move according to your flesh, you will be headed for destruction. Let me keep it real. A lot of these marriages (those in ministry and beyond) were not formed by God but by our flesh. If a person is desperate, has low self-esteem, is lonely, in need of sex, or so many other things, it can lead them into the wrong arms. That is why it is so important to not be so caught up in the moment that you might miss your moment of meeting the mate that God has for you. When you are caught up in the moment, it is hard to see clearly the real person behind the mask they are wearing. That person will make love to your mind through deception, and for some witchcraft, and it can cause you to not see who is behind it all—the adversary. If that person is in a spiritual leadership position, they can easily use their influence as a leader to make false promises that will never be fulfilled along with many other things. This level of deception can easily happen when we ignore the red flags and continue with these spiritual leaders. This too has caused chaos in the church.

When you see spiritual leaders that claim to be of God but are displaying the devil, it is hard to tell whose side they are on. When a pastor and his wife break up in ministry, it can and will hurt the congregation deeply. Not only has the married couple made a covenant with God, but also those that are in their church. When married couples are at the helm of a church, the members trust that they have it together. Therefore, leaders must be on one accord. The two of them must serve the same God. I have seen many people leave God because of a leader's mistakes.

If you are someone who desires to be married, make sure you pray before you get married, and most definitely pray before you go into ministry. Also, look at yourself and make sure you are healed and have no hidden motives for wanting to be married. You will need to make sure God is the One who will be joining you together, because the unseen truth will be revealed. With all that is currently happening in marriages and has happened in marriages that have ended in divorce, you cannot be so quick to accept a ring when it is presented to you because you are in too deep with someone and "head over heels" for them—that certain someone may not be the one God has for you. You do not want to take on challenges that could paralyze you permanently by marrying the wrong person. You must understand that what you get into is not only going to affect you, but if you have children, it could also have a negative impact on their lives. As you go through negative things in your marriage that can strip you and cause you to spiritually die and become bitter, too, your children can also experience that. You see, one way that you can tell there is a problem in the home of a spiritual leader is to look at the reaction of their children.

Some of these cunning spiritual leaders are manipulating women and men into marriage and using them for self-gain for ministry as well as marriage. Some of them may say "they have a choice," and they do but you do not understand the power, control, and influence one can have over those that are truly vulnerable. These kinds of activities in ministry and marriage

51

are frowned upon. Let me explain something: there must be a stop to the madness that is being accepted in the church.

A PASTOR'S CRY

Many would think that it would be a blessing to be married to someone in ministry that flows in the same spiritual gifts as you do. The question is, "Who are the spiritual gifts being used for and are you both serving the same God?" If the marriage is not from God, your gifts can become a weapon to the person you are with. In other words, you can be married to your very assassin. The very one that said, "God said you were their spouse" was sent by Satan to kill the God in you. You will know the signs because there will be competition, jealousy, anger, bitterness, and when God uses you, there will be no support. You will find yourself praying alone, fasting alone, eventually being alone while married. An enemy-sent spouse will snare you with lies and later become a hater of your very destiny. Who is at work here? If you are married, make sure that you are with your God-given mate and if you are not married, make sure when you get married, you marry the person that God has for you.

As a wife, I found myself having to fight to survive at home and at church. The spirit of control had overflowed from home to church. I was unable to be what I was ordained to be, and it caused people to not have respect for me at church. The person that ordain me made themselves the pastor of the church, and people saw him as the leader instead of me. Not everyone, because some generally loved me dearly, yet some of them had their agenda and wanted my place and fought me when I preached, prophesied, prayed, or did anything in the church that I was supposed to be the pastor of. They wanted me to fulfill the duties of a pastor when they needed help, and their purpose for this was to silence me. I could not go forth as God led me, and when I did they would call me before the church to make it seem as though I was not led by God in my movements in the spirit.

You can be married to the enemy and because the enemy has access to your life, it is easy for Satan to divide the marriage that God never joined. The goal of the enemy is to silence you, control you, to cause you to feel low and beneath everyone else, to put you in a stage of totally losing out with God. They are the lethal weapon designed to kill you and they were sent at the time of your vulnerability to hold you captive. They pray day and night to make sure you fail in anything you are called to do, while secretly slandering you because when they have finished with you they want an alibi for why things went wrong.

I was not fulfilled at home or in the ministry. I was dying right in front of everyone and no one caught me but my mother and a pastor friend of mine that loves me like a daughter. Many were jealous and was ready for me to pack up and exit but what they did not know was that God was laying foundations for His power to be seen through me during it all. If you do not wait on God, you will find yourself dead while still living. This is chaos in ministry and marriage.

A FIRST LADY'S CRY (THE PASTOR'S WIFE)

There are so many first ladies (pastor's wives) who have silent cries because their husbands can only see their desires and do not notice that their wives have willingly given up their lives so that they can bloom. Some first ladies' dreams have been put on hold for the ministry. They are carrying their husbands and the church. Most of their problems are put on their wives and yet some people do not want them to have a voice. They want direct access to the pastor and ignore their wives, not knowing what they are suffering and have lost to uphold their husband's image. Then you have these side birds' pieces, also known as side chicks, that see the glamour, but do not know the anointing that flows through some pastors come from the nights that some first ladies have cried and walked the floor for God to change their husbands. These first ladies bear the pain that shows over the years and yet no one sees their pain but rather adds pressure to ensure that they give up and leave it all. These first ladies are hated by many, especially these flying birds' pieces (both young and old) that want their husbands. Some of them have had to deal with jealous witches that come into the church to fight their marriage. If you are the wife of a pastor, I want you to know that God never designed for you to be a slave. You are supposed to be loved, appreciated, and respected by your husband and everyone else. You were called to be a helpmate in everything, but not to die while helping.

Let me break down how I was a first lady in my marriage and the deceit I encountered in ministry. My hope and prayer are to help first ladies understand if they want to be saved for real, and I am not just talking about being saved in God, but I am talking about being saved from the hell that some of them experience every day. Too many first ladies are simply being quiet to protect their husbands and the people of their church when in fact they are dying. Some first ladies have been treated so badly by their husbands who are pastors and the church members. With these kinds of treatment, it has caused many first ladies to start sleeping with other men and women. Jezebel is running loose in the church and the pastor will not stop that demon but rather make them a secretary, an usher, a praise leader, or assign them to some position that he works closely with.

First ladies, did you know that if you support your husband in his mess, you are considered a partaker of his actions? You are strengthening the hand of the wicked. If you know your husband is sleeping with the musician and most of the women and men in the church and you just stay there and endure it like it is God's will, then you need help. You must know that God will never join you with someone who is going to bring you down. God knows the heart and future of that person, and He will never put you in harm's way. He knows if that person has an issue in their heart, and if it is going to destroy you in the future. God looks out for your now and your future. Be honest and stop covering up for these demons in collars. Come out of hell and use your experience to help build up and support other women that are stuck in unhealthy marriages. You were built to experience real love from your husband. You were not called to be joined to a man that is living a double life and that is contaminating you and the church he is serving headship over.

I learned that I was married to the wrong person, and most of you know that you are married to the wrong one but will not admit it because you are in too deep emotionally. Why wait 20 years of your life for someone to change? God did not put the marriage together but rather your fleshly desires and therefore you are in an unhealthy marriage. I was too. Yes, many have had sex before marriage and have gotten into a relationship with those who were already married and claiming to have gotten a divorce. Once we found out they were lying, we stayed anyway. It started wrong and ended wrong. Ministry for a first lady is complicated, and I certainly understand it all too well. A man or woman that does not know their identity is dangerous.

THE TESTIMONY

Now that I have described the chaos in ministry and marriage, I need to encourage someone that feels trapped and cannot get out of this kind of relationship. God is so merciful, and He hears a person's inner cry. He will deliver. I cried so many tears and prayed so many nights. I remember just before I left the marriage and the ministry, I got in my car and drove for miles with tears streaming down my face. I told God that I was ready to go. God heard my prayers and not many weeks after that He gave me clear instructions. My spiritual father was on Facebook live, and at that time, I was not connected to him. He prophesied to me and told me that God wanted me to go on a fast and after the fast, I would experience a breakthrough. I went on a 21-day fast, and one day I woke up and the Lord told me to go now. I used the car and dropped my ex-husband off, and I went straight home and got my kids and my grandson and hit the road, leaving everything I owned. All I had was a bag of clothes. God brought me out of that marriage. I was bound in that marriage and the ministry. The abuse, tears, jealousy, hatred, and lack in every way was over. I was driving down the road of freedom. The process after it all was a mind battle, but even in that, God brought me out. If God allowed me to walk away from all this, He can certainly do it for those of you who may be bound in a marriage like this, too.

There is no kind of situation or circumstance that God cannot bring you out of. Nothing is too hard for Him. I was dying both naturally and spiritually. Your soul is far more important than a relationship or ministry that may be killing you. No more desiring something that would have never been. No more fights. You can let go. Once you make up your mind, it will not be hard to let go of anything that will steal your peace and time with God. Be free in the name of Jesus.

TAKEAWAYS AND PERSONAL NOTES FOR SPIRITUAL GROWTH

_____

_____

_____

_____

_____

_____

_____

_____

_____

_____

_____

_____

_____

_____

_____

_____

_____

_____

_____

_____

_____

_____

_____

THE TARE AND THE WHEAT

It is easy for some people to say "I am a Christian," or just be religious, but their hearts are far from doing what is Christ-like. In this book, I have shared some things that commonly happen in the church world. I wanted to make it noticeably clear how the body of Christ (Christians who are in Christ) is moving in the right direction, but there are some people who have been referred to as tares throughout this book, that have caused chaos in some churches and, because of this, have affected those who are vulnerable. This has also caused unsaved people who do not go to church to have a negative outlook on the church and Christians as a whole. It is the tares that have performed the works of evil, but the entire body of Christ has been labeled for its wrong. The tares come to steal, kill, and destroy, just like their father, the devil. Everyone that is not of the Kingdom of God will prey on those who attend church and living for God. Many people have lost their lives and have given up on the Lord because of the tares. Many of their minds have been damaged.

In an effort to expose the tares and dismantle the devil's tactics that have been carried out by the tares, we must simply sit back and "Let both grow together until harvest, and at the time of harvest I will say to the reapers, 'First gather together the tares and bind them in bundles to burn them, but gather the wheat into my barn" (Matthew 13:30-NJJV). God will do the separation and it is happening right now. God is calling for His true body to get ready for His coming. We will never have to worry about the tares again, because God will settle the case. No more shall we allow the kingdom of darkness to look like us, but the glory of God is about to show the difference just like He did with the children of Israel and the Egyptians (Read Exodus 14:13). The body of Christ is not them and the tares are not us.

The body of Christ has never and will never be a part of the deceptive movement, but we have been sound in all that God has called us to be. We are living for God and have no desire to be a part of any church world mess. We have made some mistakes, but we are not committed to the kingdom of darkness. We are committed to making a difference in the lives of those who we come in contact with in this world, and we are also committed to advancing the Kingdom of God. We are striving to someday hear these words: "Well done, good and faithful servant" (Matthew 25:21).

ENCOURAGING WORDS

Even though we are walking through the shadows of death, we shall fear no evil (Psalm 23). Everything concerning us has already been established in Heaven before we were born; therefore, we attach not ourselves to the things of this world that would keep us blinded in deception, but we press forward toward purpose that was destined for our existence in the earth realm. I want to encourage you to keep reaching for your crown that is laid before you. Allow God to guide you, through His spirit on your earthly journey. Do good and good things will follow you. Do not be discouraged by the things you see or the things the enemy magnifies in your sight. I understand the challenges that are ahead but through Christ you can do all things. Philippians 4:13-KJV states, "I can do all things through Christ which strengthens me." I would like to challenge you, to acknowledge the shaded areas in your life, and pursue eliminating any possible threat to your salvation. Romans 8:37 declares, "You are more than a conquer through Christ Jesus."

ABOUT THE AUTHOR

Pastor Tomica Scott is the second generation of preachers in her family and has impacted many around the world. She was saved and committed herself to Jesus Christ at the age 21, and she has not looked back. She served at a church under the leadership of her biological mother for years. She later expanded and launched her own ministry in 2017. She is the Pastor of All Jesus Ministries in Dallas, Texas. She is also the founder of *Woman Be Healed Now* in both Dallas, Texas, and Birmingham, Alabama. As a leader, she has experienced being traumatized by some churches. She is in full pursuit of making the Kingdom of God conscious of the devil's devices. She operates heavily in deliverance and in teaching the Word of God.

PERSONAL NOTES

_____

_____

_____

_____

_____

_____

_____

_____

_____

_____

_____

_____

_____

_____

_____

_____

_____

_____

_____

PERSONAL NOTES

_____

_____

_____

_____

_____

_____

_____

_____

_____

_____

_____

_____

_____

_____

_____

_____

_____

_____

_____

_____

_____

_____

PERSONAL NOTES

PERSONAL NOTES

_____

_____

_____

_____

_____

_____

_____

_____

_____

_____

_____

_____

_____

_____

_____

_____

_____

_____

_____

_____

_____

PERSONAL NOTES

_____

_____

_____

_____

_____

_____

_____

_____

_____

_____

_____

_____

_____

_____

_____

_____

_____

_____

_____

_____

_____

PERSONAL NOTES

_____
_____
_____
_____
_____
_____
_____
_____
_____
_____
_____
_____
_____
_____
_____
_____
_____
_____
_____
_____
_____

PERSONAL NOTES

_____

_____

_____

_____

_____

_____

_____

_____

_____

_____

_____

_____

_____

_____

_____

_____

_____

_____

_____

_____

PERSONAL NOTES

_____

_____

_____

_____

_____

_____

_____

_____

_____

_____

_____

_____

_____

_____

_____

_____

_____

_____

_____

_____

_____

PERSONAL NOTES

_____

_____

_____

_____

_____

_____

_____

_____

_____

_____

_____

_____

_____

_____

_____

_____

_____

_____

_____

_____

_____

PERSONAL NOTES

PERSONAL NOTES

PERSONAL NOTES

_____

_____

_____

_____

_____

_____

_____

_____

_____

_____

_____

_____

_____

_____

_____

_____

_____

_____

_____

_____

PERSONAL NOTES

_____

_____

_____

_____

_____

_____

_____

_____

_____

_____

_____

_____

_____

_____

_____

_____

_____

_____

_____

PERSONAL NOTES